D0985581

# THE PRAYERS OF SAINT FRANCIS

# The Prayers of Saint Francis

*Francis of Assisi*

Translated by
Ignatius Brady O.F.M.

SERVANT BOOKS
Ann Arbor, Michigan

Copyright © 1988 by The Franciscan Friars of St. John the
Baptist Province
All rights reserved.

Prayers in this book are taken from *The Writings of
St. Francis*, translated by Ignatius Brady O.F.M.
(Rome: Edizioni Porziuncola, 1983).

Published by Servant Books
P.O. Box 8617
Ann Arbor, Michigan 48107

Cover painting by P.J. Lynch; Brighton, England
Cover design Michael Andaloro
Text design Beth Parr

Printed in the United States of America
ISBN 0-89283-386-6

91 92   10 9 8 7 6 5

# Contents

# Foreword

In 1983 I recorded an album for Sparrow Records entitled "Troubadour for the Great King" in honor of the eighth centenary of St. Francis. In that musical work I used many of the medieval prayers of St. Francis as texts for the melodies of my simple prayer songs. I am grateful that the album went on to be a best-seller among Christians throughout the world.

It pleases me to see many of these same prayers in this edition translated by the renowned Franciscan scholar, Ignatius Brady, O.F.M. The prayers themselves speak across the ages. They continue to instruct and inspire many Christians from a wide array of circumstances, lifestyles, and cultures who, like St. Francis, try to live out the gospel of Jesus Christ.

Father Brady's introduction to the life of St. Francis and to each of his prayers is of great help as we try to apply the prayers of an Italian medieval saint to the realities of our modern world. St. Francis said, "I have done my part, may Christ teach you yours." I hope this book of thirteenth century prayers will help you open yourself to Jesus Christ today. Of course, we all can do this under the ultimate inspiration of the timeless and eternal Holy Spirit of Jesus, who St. Francis called "the minister general of the whole order."

It is my desire that, just as my musical rendition of many of these prayers of St. Francis reached many Christians and non-Christians alike with the simple gospel, so this book will draw many hungry souls to Christ. With music, the words easily enter past the mind to the heart of the listener. But without some effort by the reader, the printed word does not as easily penetrate the heart. I encourage you to read these prayers, not so much as intellectual investigations into the spirituality of St. Francis, but as your own personal prayer. These words must be meditated, not merely read.

I am reminded of St. Bonaventure's words: "since nature is powerless in this regard, and effort of slight avail, little importance should be given to investigation, but much to affection; little to speech, but more to joy; little to words and writings, but all to the Gift of God, the Holy Spirit." Or again, "Let us not believe that it is enough to read without unction. Prayer, then, is the mother and the beginning of the ascent." So, it is my hope that this book of prayers will lead you to personal prayer, so that by prayer leading to prayer, all will lead to Christ.

John Michael Talbot

# Introduction

One of the most intriguing stories about Saint Francis (which in all likelihood is not pure legend) places him in the woods that once surrounded the little church of the Porziuncola. Returning from prayer, he is met at the edge of the forest by his companion, Brother Masseo of Marignano, who seeks to discover how humble Francis really is. Teasingly Brother Masseo cries out to him: "Why after you? Why after you? Why after you?" A bit bewildered, Francis answers: "What are you trying to say? What do you mean?" "This," Masseo replies: "Why does all the world seem to be running after you and wanting to see you and hear you and obey you? You're not a very handsome man; you don't have great learning or wisdom! You're not of noble blood! So why is it that all the world is coming to you?"

Caught up in God, Francis eventually answers Masseo: "You want to know why after me? Why? Because God did not find a greater sinner than me or one more simple and foolish, and so he chose me because he has chosen the foolish things of the world to put to shame the wise, and the base things of the world to bring to naught the noble and great and strong!"

Small wonder then that Brother Masseo was deeply moved by such an answer and was thus reassured that Saint Francis was grounded in genuine humility and was in very truth the lowly disciple of Christ.

## Who Was Francis of Assisi?

At the end of the twelfth century one might have asked whether any good could come out of Assisi, torn as it was by factions within and rivalry without, especially against nearby Perugia. But at the end of the thirteenth century people of many nations could but wonder at the change God had worked not only in that town but throughout Europe as well and, indeed, in far-distant lands, through Saint Francis and his many holy followers. From what we know of Assisi when the Lady Pica gave birth (about 1182) to the first of two sons, no great future could be predicted for the town or for him, later legends notwithstanding. Religion was more of a habit and tradition than of genuine conviction; political conditions were unstable, in part because of constant friction between the higher class and the ordinary citizens. Yet in the providence of God that son, baptized John while his father, Pietro di Bernardone, was absent in France on the business of a cloth merchant, and then dubbed Francis by the father, was eventually to be the man who would awaken and rejuvenate Assisi (and, indeed, much of Italy) and bring the people back to God.

What an unlikely choice, from our point of view! His first biographer, Friar Thomas of Celano, was to say quite bluntly that young Francis proved more of an adventurer than the son of a cloth merchant, a young man who wasted the first twenty-five years of his life in dreams of greatness. At the same time, Thomas does admit that Francis was also affable and thoughtful of others.

At twenty (late in the year 1202), he deemed himself ready for great things. He would ride, fully accoutered in the finest armor, astride the best horse Assisi could provide, to win honors for himself against the enemy, the citizens of the nearby town of Perugia. The battle (in November 1202) took place at Collestrada, along the road to Perugia. The enemy was stronger, and the Assisians who were not killed were captured (Francis among them) and ignominiously thrown into prison at Perugia.

Sick in body as well as in spirit, the would-be hero was ransomed at last, but he was still weak for months to come. Yet his convalescence does not seem to have dampened his chivalrous desire to become a great knight. Indeed, once again in good health, he planned to join, with others from Assisi, the troops of Walter of Brienne, leader of the papal forces of

Innocent III in southern Italy.

At this point the Lord intervened. The first step in his new life was an act of generosity toward a poor but noble knight in rags and tatters. Francis exchanges garments with him as Saint Martin had done in times long past for an unfortunate beggar. As his reward, he dreams that his father's house becomes a palace in which a most beautiful bride, Lady Poverty, awaits him.

Still a man of the world, however, Francis departed for southern Italy and the knights of the papal army under the command of Walter of Brienne. At the end of the first day he took lodging at Spoleto, only to hear a voice in the night which asked him what he planned to do. When he explained that he wanted to go to Apuglia (on the east coast of the boot of Italy) to join the papal troops, a further question was put to him: "Who is more important, the servant or the Master?" When he answered: "The Master," he was told: "Why then do you seek the servant instead of the Master? Go home, for what I have shown you in the vision [of the palace] will be fulfilled in you by me, but in a spiritual way."

When he reached Assisi, he shrugged off questions about his joy of spirit, playfully declaring that he would become a great prince. In reality, it was the beginning of his conversion. He began to pray in a cave near the town, asking the Lord of glory to direct his steps and teach him to do his will, for he was unsure of himself, so unaccustomed was he to the ways of God. Little by little he came to know what the Lord wanted of him: victory over self, abandonment of family and friends, money and worldly honor, in a life centered on God alone. If we read his *Testament*, dictated to Brother Leo shortly before his death, we get some glimpse of the change that took place within him and the new pattern of life which he and the brothers who flocked to him began to lead, in faith, in prayer, in poverty.

A turning point in his new life was surely the visit he made to the ruined church of San Damiano in Assisi, which for long had been abandoned. He knelt before the image of Christ crucified. Suddenly the lips moved and a voice said: "Francis, repair my house which, as you see, is completely in ruins." Wholly astonished at such a command, and not a little shaken, he set about to do as he was commanded. And as he did, he felt a great change within himself: his heart, his whole being, was caught up to Christ in love, and thereafter he could never think or speak of Christ crucified without weeping. The church he thus repaired was to become, a few years later, the first home of Lady Clare and her early followers (1212), as

Francis himself had earlier prophesied. A second church, dedicated to Saint Peter and restored by Francis, seems lost in history. The third, Our Lady of the Angels, is to be found under the dome of the great Basilica of the Porziuncola. It soon became the center for Francis and the growing number of those who came to join the Lesser Brothers, the Friars Minor. It was there that Francis died at sundown on Saturday, October 3 (or according to the Umbrian way of calculating the day from sundown, in the first hours of October 4).

The intervening years had indeed been blessed by the Lord. Other men of Assisi and the neighboring towns had early been drawn to follow Francis and leave all for Christ. They were soon joined by others from all parts of Italy and, somewhat later, from almost the whole of Europe. Before long, led by the zeal and example of Francis, they went forth to bring new life to Christians or sought to bring the faith to unbelievers. In 1220, five were martyred in Morocco; Francis himself and others went to the East and possibly to the Holy Land; somewhere, he met the Sultan himself.

His real goal was martyrdom, but the Lord did not grant him that grace. He was to return to Assisi to write a new Rule of Life for the brothers, eventually approved in revised form by Pope Honorius III (1223); to celebrate the birth of Christ at what was perhaps the first Christmas crib (Greccio 1223); and to be signed with the wounds of Christ (the stigmata) in hands and feet and side on Mount La Verna (1224).

The following year, warned by severe illnesses of his approaching death, he revealed his inner spirit of joy when in a hut at San Damiano, by now the flourishing convent of Saint Clare and her Poor Ladies, he composed the Canticle of Brother Sun, as well as another Song for the encouragement and consolation of the Sisters. Both were an expression of his desire always to give glory to the "Most High, Omnipotent, Good Lord" in all circumstances of life.

A tiring journey (in 1225-1226) to San Fabiano and then to Siena, to consult physicians regarding his eyes, brought no relief. When he returned to Assisi, he rested in the palace of the bishop for some months, and there dictated his Testament to Brother Leo. A precious document in which he recalls and celebrates the graces given him by the Lord from his conversion to his last days, it is at the same time an earnest exhortation to his Brothers to be faithful to their calling, to the Order and to the Rule, to love and venerate the church and the papacy, to have faith and confidence in her priests, reverence and love for the Eucharist, and total fidelity and concern for the people of God.

A few days before his death, Francis was brought from the palace to his beloved Porziuncola, since he wished to die there, in the Little Portion that the Lord had given him on this earth. Some years after his death, Brother Leo gave a vivid portrait of the life and death of the Seraphic Saint to the Franciscan writer and chronicler, Salimbene of Parma (d. 1288), who later wrote: "Never in the history of this whole world was there anyone other than the Blessed Francis on whom Christ imprinted the five wounds in likeness to himself. For, as Brother Leo, his companion, who was present when his body was washed for burial, told me, Francis truly seemed like a man who had been crucified and taken down from the cross."

From the Porziuncola that worn-out body was carried for burial to the Church of Saint George, where as a young lad he had been taught the rudiments of faith, where indeed he had learned to read and write, and where much later he had begun to preach. In the same little church, on Sunday, July 16, 1228, he was canonized by Pope Gregory IX, who as friend and protector had known and loved Francis. Later, on May 25, 1230, his sacred remains were transferred to the Basilica which had been built in his honor, a holy place frequented ever since by all pilgrims to Assisi.

## Our Edition

Essentially, this book presents the prayers of Saint Francis, each with a brief introduction to put it in proper perspective.

More than once Francis apologized because his writing is simple in style and totally unadorned. In reality, these prayers are more often gems of true Christian wisdom. God works indeed in mysterious ways his lessons to impart: indeed, the Prayers of Saint Francis truly bear the imprint of the Holy Spirit, who drew the whole world after Francis.

Ignatius Brady O.F.M.

# ONE

# A Prayer
# before the Crucifix

The first biographer of Saint Francis, Thomas of Celano, says bluntly that for the first twenty-five years of his life Francis wasted his time on the vanities of the world. Then touched by the grace of God, he called upon the Lord to show him what he was to do. His cry for help is expressed in this prayer, especially in its simpler form (1). Another, slightly different form, in use in the English-speaking world, corresponds to the text as published by the Irish Franciscan historian Luke Wadding (2).

# A Prayer
# before the Crucifix

### 1

*O most high, glorious God, enlighten the darkness of my heart and give me a right faith, a certain hope and a perfect love, understanding and knowledge, O Lord, that I may carry out your holy and true command.*

### 2

*O great and glorious God and my Lord Jesus Christ, enlighten, I beseech thee, the darkness of my mind. Give me a right faith, a certain hope, and a perfect charity. Grant that I may know thee, Lord, in order that I may always and in all things act according to thy most holy and perfect will. Amen.*

# TWO

# The Canticle
# of Brother Sun

A note in the Assisi manuscript 338, folio 33, reads: "Here begins the Praises of the Creatures which the Blessed Francis made to the Praise and Honor of God while he was ill in San Damiano." The Canticle is truly the climax of a life of praise of the Creator; indeed, Thomas of Cela says that as the three youths in the fiery furnace called upon the elements to praise and glorify the Creator of all, so Saint Francis, filled with the spirit of God, never ceased to glorify, praise and bless the Creator and Lord of all in all elements and creatures. Translations in English are often at fault, for this is not a song about creatures, but a joyful praise of the Lord composed by a saint who in the midst of great suffering retained a heart full of joy in the Lord, and then at the end added the verse on Sister Death, to die with such a song on his lips and in his heart.

# The Canticle
# of Brother Sun

Most high, omnipotent, good Lord,
To you alone, Most High, do they
  belong,
And there is no one worthy to mention
  you.
Praised be my Lord,
by means of all your creatures,
and most especially by Sir Brother Sun,
Who makes the day and illumines us by
  his light:
For he is beautiful and radiant with
  great splendor;
And is a symbol of you, God most high.
Praised be my Lord,
by means of Sister Moon and all the
  stars:
For in heaven you have placed them,
clear, precious, and fair.
Praised be my Lord, by means of

Brother Wind,
And by means of the air, the clouds,
and the clear sky and every kind of
    weather,
through which you give your creatures
    nourishment.
Praised be my Lord, by means of Sister
    Water:
For she is very useful, humble, precious
    and chaste.
Praised be my Lord, by means of Brother
    Fire,
By whom you do illumine the night:
For he is fair and gay and mighty and
    strong.
Praised be my Lord,
by means of our sister Mother Earth,
Which sustains us and keeps us,
And brings forth varied fruits
with colored flowers and leaves.
Praised be my Lord,
through those who give pardon for love
    of you,
And suffer infirmity and tribulation.
Blessed are they who endure all in
    peace,
For they, O God most high,

will be crowned by you.
Praised be my Lord, through our sister
  Bodily Death,
From whom no living person can
  escape.
Woe to those who die in mortal sin!
But blessed are those found in your
  most holy will,
For the second death will do them no
  harm.
Praise and bless my Lord,
And thank him, and serve him with
  great humility.

# THREE

# Praises of the Lord God Most High

This prayer is found on a scroll given to Brother Leo, written by Saint Francis himself. On the reverse side of the parchment, which is preserved in the Sacro Convento (San Francesco), Assisi, is found, in the handwriting of St. Francis, the blessing for Brother Leo.

# *Praises of the Lord God Most High*

*You are the holy Lord, the only God,*
  *who work wonders.*
*You are strong. You are great. You are*
  *most high.*
*You are the Almighty King, you, O Holy*
  *Father,*
*King of heaven and earth,*
*You are three and one, the Lord God of*
  *gods;*
*You are good, all good, the highest good,*
*Lord God, living and true.*
*You are love, charity.*
*You are wisdom, you are humility,*
*You are patience, you are beauty.*
*You are meekness, you are security.*
*You are quietude, you are joy.*
*You are our hope and gladness.*
*You are justice, you are temperance.*
*You are all our riches to the full.*

You are beauty, you are meekness.
You are protector, you are our guardian
and defender;
You are strength, you are refreshment.
You are our hope, you are our faith,
You are our charity; you are all our
delight.
You are our eternal life:
The great and wondrous Lord,
God Almighty, merciful Savior!

# FOUR

# The Blessing
# for Brother Leo

Brother Leo himself made some annotations on the parchment on which this prayer is found:

1. In the upper margin we read:

"Brother Francis two years before his death kept a Lent in the place of La Verna in honor of the Blessed Virgin Mary, the Mother of God, and of Saint Michael, from the feast of the Assumption of the holy Virgin Mary until the September feast of Saint Michael. After the vision and words of the seraph and the impression of the stigmata of Christ in his body he made these praises written on the other side of this sheet and wrote in his own hand, giving thanks to God for the grace bestowed on him."

2. Below the Blessing Leo wrote: "The Blessed Francis wrote with his own hand this blessing for me, Brother Leo."

3. At the lower part of the parchment is a *Tau* with a head (that is, a T with a skull) from the hand of Saint Francis, as Leo notes: "In like manner with his own hand he made this sign, the Tau, and the skull."

# The Blessing
# for Brother Leo

May the Lord bless thee and keep thee;
May he show his face to thee and have
   mercy on thee.
May he turn his countenance to thee
   and give thee peace
The Lord bless thee, Brother Leo.

# FIVE

# An Exhortation to Praise God

Franciscan chronicles (of Marianus of Florence and the Annals of Luke Wadding) speak of a wooden antipendium (or front) attached to an altar in the ancient Franciscan hermitage at Cesi di Terni (midway between Rome and Assisi) on which Saint Francis himself wrote verses of Scripture calling on creatures to praise their Creator. Though the original piece has disappeared, the texts Saint Francis wrote have been found in a manuscript in Naples as copied by a fifteenth-century witness from the original antipendium which by then was attached to the wall of the chapel.

# An Exhortation
# to Praise God

*Fear the Lord and give him honor.*
*The Lord is worthy to receive*
*praise and honor.*
*All you who fear the Lord, praise him.*
*Hail Mary, full of grace,*
*the Lord is with you.*
*Praise him,*
*heaven and earth.*
*Praise the Lord, all ye rivers.*
*All you children of God, bless the Lord.*
*This is the day the Lord has made:*
*let us be glad and rejoice therein.*
*Response: Alleluia, Alleluia, Alleluia,*
*O King of Israel.*
*Let everything that has breath*
*Praise the Lord.*
*Praise the Lord, for he is good.*
*All you who read this, bless the Lord.*
*All creatures bless the Lord.*

*All you birds of the air, bless the Lord.*
*All you children, praise the Lord.*
*Young men and maidens, praise the*
*Lord.*
*Worthy is the Lamb that was slain*
*to receive praise, glory, and honor.*
*Blessed be the Holy Trinity and*
*undivided Unity.*
*Saint Michael the Archangel, defend us*
*in battle.*

# SIX

# The Salutation
# to Our Lady

Thomas of Celano, the early biographer, says that Francis loved the Mother of Jesus with a love beyond all telling because she made the Lord of majesty our Brother; thus he composed special praises in her honor (*The Second Life*, n. 198).

# The Salutation to Our Lady

Hail, O Lady, Holy Queen, God's Holy
  Mother Mary!
You have been made the virgin church
And chosen by the most holy Father in
  heaven.
You has he consecrated with his most
  holy beloved Son
and the Holy Spirit the Paraclete.
In you there has been, and is,
all fullness of grace, and all that is
  good.
Hail his Palace! Hail his Tabernacle!
Hail his Dwelling Place!
Hail his Garment! Hail his Handmaid!
Hail his Mother!
And hail all you holy virtues in her
  which by the
grace and enlightenment of the
  Holy Spirit

are poured forth into the hearts of the
   faithful,
that from faithless souls
You may make them faithful to God!

# SEVEN

# Salutation
# of the Virtues

Thomas of Celano vouches for the authenticity of this delightful song of praise to the virtues, since he cites the opening verse in his *Second Life* of Saint Francis, n. 189, as he portrays the true simplicity of Saint Francis and its meaning for all who follow him. Two manuscripts link the virtues here praised with Mary: "On the virtues which adorned the Holy Virgin and should be in every holy soul." When Saint Francis composed this prayer cannot be determined.

# Salutation
# of the Virtues

*Hail, Queen Wisdom! May the Lord*
   *preserve you*
*with your sister holy pure Simplicity!*
*O lady holy Poverty, may the Lord save*
   *you*
*with your sister holy Humility!*
*O lady holy Charity, may the Lord save*
   *you*
*with your sister holy Obedience!*
*O all you most holy virtues,*
*may the Lord save you all,*
*from Whom you come and proceed.*
*There is truly no man in the whole*
   *world*
*who can possess one of you unless he*
   *first die*
*to self.*
*He who has one and does not offend the*
   *others,*

possesses all;
And he who offends one,
possesses none and offends all.
And each of them puts to rout vices and
  sins.
Holy Wisdom confounds Satan and all
  his wicked ways.
Pure holy Simplicity confounds all the
  wisdom
of this world and the wisdom of the
  flesh.
Holy Poverty confounds cupidity and
  avarice
and the cares of this world.
Holy Humility confounds pride
and all the people who are in this world
and in like manner all things that are in
  the world.
Holy Charity confounds all temptations
  that come from
the devil or from the flesh, and all
  human fears.
Holy Obedience puts to rout
all self-centered and carnal desires
and keeps the body subject to the
  obedience
of the inner man and to obedience to

one's brother,
and thus a man is subject and
    submissive to all men
who are in the world; and not only to
    humans, but
also to all beasts and wild animals, so
    that they may
do with him whatsoever they will,
    insofar as it may
have been granted them from above by
    the Lord.

# EIGHT

# The Explanation
# of the Our Father

A recent list of commentaries on the Our Father by mediaeval writers (F. Stegmuller-N. Reinhardt, Repertorium Biblicum XI, pp. 191-201) contains some 330 or more entries, including the Explanation by Saint Francis as found in a codex in Brussels. Who acted as scribe or secretary of Saint Francis cannot be ascertained; yet he is possessed of some patristic background, inasmuch as the phrase "in the angels and in the saints" is found in a ninth-century paraphrase of the Our Father.

# The Explanation of the Our Father

O most holy Pater noster: *our Creator,
Redeemer, Consoler, and Savior.*
Who art in heaven: *in the angels and in
the saints; enlightening them to know
[you], for you, O Lord, are light;
enkindling them to love, for you, O
Lord, are love; dwelling in them and
filling them with happiness, because
you, Lord, are the highest Good, the
[eternal] Good, from whom is every
good; without whom there is no good.*
Hallowed be your name: *may our
knowledge of you ever increase in
clarity, that we may know what is the
breadth of your gifts, the length of your
promises, the heights of your majesty,
and the depth of your judgements.*
Your kingdom come: *that you may reign
in us through grace and make us come*

to your kingdom where there is clear
vision of you, perfect love of you,
blessed union with you, [and]
everlasting enjoyment of you.
Your will be done on earth as it is in
heaven: to the end that we may love
you with our whole heart by always
thinking of you; with our whole soul by
ever desiring you; with our whole mind
by directing all our intentions to you,
by seeking your honor in all things; and
with all our strength by spending all our
powers and senses of body and soul in
the service of your love and in nought
else; and that we may love our
neighbors even as ourselves, drawing all
to your love to the best of our power;
rejoicing in the good of others as in our
own and compassionating them in their
troubles and giving no offence to
anyone.
Give us this day our daily bread: your
beloved Son, our Lord Jesus Christ, that
we may keep in mind and understand
and revere the love which he had for us,
and all that he taught us and did and
suffered for us.

And forgive us our trespasses: *out of your ineffable mercy, through the power of the Passion of your beloved Son, and through the merits and intercession of the most Blessed Virgin and of all your elect.*

As we forgive those who trespass against us: *and what we do not fully forgive, do you, O Lord, make us forgive in full, that we may truly love [our] enemies for your sake and devotedly intercede for them before you, not rendering anyone evil for evil, but in you may strive to be of help to all.*

And lead us not into temptation, *hidden or evident, sudden or persistent.*

But deliver us from evil, *past, present, or to come.*

*Glory to the Father. . . .*

# NINE

# Praises to Be Said at Each of the Hours of the Office

"These are the Praises which the Blessed Francis put together" from sacred Scripture and the Liturgy, "and was wont to say before all the Hours" [of the Office]. The manuscripts would indicate that these Praises followed the Explanation of the Our Father: "O most holy *Pater noster*: our Creator, Redeemer . . ." which is Chapter Eight of this edition.

# Praises to Be Said at Each of the Hours of the Office

Holy, holy, holy, is the Lord God
   Almighty,
He who is, and who was, and who is to
   come.
And let us praise and exalt him above
   all for ever!
You are worthy, O Lord our God, to
   receive praise,
glory and honor and blessing:
and let us praise and exalt him above all
   forever!
The Lamb that was slain is worthy to
   receive power,
and divinity and wisdom and strength,
and honor and glory and blessing.
And let us praise and exalt him above
   all for ever!

Let us bless the Father and the Son
with the Holy Spirit:
And let us praise and exalt him above
all forever!
All you works of the Lord, bless the
Lord!
And let us praise and exalt him above
all forever!
Give praise to our God, all you his
servants,
And you who revere God,
the little and the great!
And let us praise and exalt him above
all forever!
Let the heavens and the earth praise
him,
the glorious One:
And let us praise and exalt him above
all forever!
And let every creature in heaven and on
the earth,
and under the earth, and the sea, and
every creature
that is in it praise him;
And let us praise and exalt him above
all forever!
Glory be to the Father and to the Son

and to the Holy Spirit:
And let us praise and exalt him above
   all forever!
As it was in the beginning, is now,
and will be forever.
Amen.

And let us praise and exalt him above
   all forever!

# Prayer

Almighty, most holy, most high and
   supreme God,
All good, the highest good, wholly good,
Who alone are good:
To you we render all praise, all glory, all
   grace,
All honor, all blessing, and everything
   that is good.
So be it! So be it! Amen!

# TEN

# The Office
# of the Passion

The introductory rubric to this Office tells us: "Here begin the Psalms which our most blessed Father Francis put together to venerate and recall to mind and to praise the Passion of the Lord. They are to be said along with the day hours [of the Office] and at the one at night [Compline]. And they begin at Compline of Good Friday [we would say, of Holy Thursday; but in the Middle Ages the new day began at sundown] because it was on that night that our Lord Jesus Christ was betrayed and taken captive. And note that the Blessed Francis was wont to say this Office thus: First he would say the prayer which the Lord and Master taught us [The Explanation of the Our Father]: 'O most holy *Pater noster*: our Creator . . .' and so on together with the Praises to Be Said at Each of the Hours of the Office which begin: 'Holy, holy, holy, is the Lord God Almighty.' When he had finished the Lauds and its prayer, he would begin this antiphon, namely 'Holy Virgin Mary.' He then said the Psalms of Mary most holy; then he said other psalms which he had chosen [verses he had put together from various psalms]; and at the end of all the psalms he would say the Psalms of the Passion [the Office here]. After each psalm [of each Hour] he said the antiphon 'Holy Virgin Mary.' The end of this antiphon was also the end of the Office."

The Office as found in the original manuscripts is in shortened form and has obscure directions on its use. Therefore, this edition has been arranged and edited to allow the modern reader to pray The Office with Saint Francis. The Psalm text is a combination of the old (Douay) version, close to the Latin of the Vulgate, and the New American Bible. At times the Jerusalem Bible also has been consulted.

# The Office
# of the Passion

**In Advent**
These psalms were arranged by Saint Francis to
be said from the beginning of Advent until the
vigil of Christmas. We have put the Hour of
Vespers first, according to modern usage; this
is followed by Compline and then the day
Hours of Matins, Prime, Tierce, Sext and
Nones.

# Vespers

*The Antiphon intoned:*
*Holy Virgin Mary*

*All you peoples, clap your hands:*
*shout to God with cries of gladness!*
*For the Lord, the most high, the*
*    awesome,*
*is the great King over all the earth.*
*Because the most holy Father of heaven,*
*our King before all ages,*
*sent his beloved Son from on high,*
*and has wrought salvation in the midst*
*    of the earth.*
*Let the heavens be glad and the earth*
*    rejoice;*
*let the sea and all that fills it be moved,*
*let the plains be joyful and all things in*
*    them.*
*Sing to the Lord a new song,*

sing to the Lord, all you lands!
For great is the Lord and highly to be
   praised:
awesome is he, beyond all gods.
Give to the Lord, you families of
   nations;
give to the Lord glory and honor:
give to the Lord the glory due his
   name!
Offer up your very selves and carry his
   holy cross
and follow to the very end his most
   holy commandments.
Glory to the Father and to the Son
and to the Holy Spirit.
As it was in the beginning,
is now, and will be forever. Amen.
The full Antiphon: Holy Virgin Mary,
there is none like you born in the world
among women, daughter and handmaid
of the most high King, the Father in
heaven! Mother of our most holy Lord
Jesus Christ! Spouse of the Holy Spirit!
Pray for us, with Saint Michael the
Archangel and all the powers of heaven
and all the saints, to your most holy
beloved Son, our Lord and Master. Glory

to the Father and to the Son and to the Holy Spirit. As it was in the beginning, is now, and will be forever. Amen.

# Compline

*The Antiphon intoned:*
*Holy Virgin Mary*

*How long, O Lord? Will you utterly*
*   forget me?*
*How long will you hide your face from*
*   me?*
*How long shall I harbor grief in my*
*   soul,*
*sorrow in my heart day after day?*
*How long will my enemy triumph over*
*   me?*
*Look and answer me, O Lord my God!*
*Give light to my eyes that I may never*
*   sleep in death,*
*lest my enemy say: I have overcome*
*   him!*
*Those who trouble me will rejoice in*
*   my downfall,*
*yet I have trusted in your mercy.*

My heart shall rejoice in your saving
    help;
I shall sing to the Lord who gives me
    good things,
and I shall praise the name of the Lord
    the most high.
Glory to the Father and to the Son
and to the Holy Spirit.
As it was in the beginning,
is now, and will be forever. Amen.
The full Antiphon: Holy Virgin Mary,
there is none like you. . . . As
concluding prayer to this Hour, Saint
Francis always said:
Let us bless the Lord God living and
true! Let us always render him praise,
glory, honor, blessing, and all good
things! Amen. Amen. So be it! So be it!

# Matins

*The Antiphon intoned:*
*Holy Virgin Mary*

*I shall give you thanks, O Lord, most*
  *holy Father,*
*King of heaven and earth,*
*because you have consoled me.*
*You are God my Savior:*
*I will be full of confidence and without*
  *fear!*
*My strength and my song is the Lord,*
*and he has become my salvation.*
*Your right hand, O Lord, is magnificent*
  *in power,*
*Your right hand, O Lord, has shattered*
  *the enemy,*
*and in the greatness of your glory*
*you have overthrown my adversaries.*
*Let the poor see and be glad:*
*Seek the Lord, and your soul shall live.*

Let the heavens and the earth praise
   him,
the sea and every thing that moves
   therein.
For God will save Zion,
and the cities of Judah shall be rebuilt.
And they shall dwell in the land,
and acquire it by inheritance.
And the descendents of his servants
   shall possess it;
and they who love his name shall dwell
   therein.
The full antiphon: Holy Virgin Mary,
there is none like you. . . .

# Prime

The Antiphon intoned:
*Holy Virgin Mary*

Have mercy on me, O God, have mercy
   on me:
for my soul trusts in you.
And in the shadow of your wings I will
   hope,
until iniquity pass away.
I will call to my most holy Father, the
   most high,
to the Lord who has done good to me.
He has sent from heaven and freed me:
He has made those a reproach who
   trampled on me.
God has sent his mercy and his
   faithfulness:
He has snatched my soul from my
   mighty enemies
and from those who hate me,

for they were too powerful for me.
They have prepared a snare for my feet,
and have bowed down my soul.
They have dug a pit before my face,
and they have fallen into it.
My heart is steadfast, O God! My heart
 is steadfast!
I will sing and chant a psalm of praise.
Awake, my soul; awake lyre and harp!
I will awake the dawn.
I will give praise to you among the
 peoples, O Lord!
I will chant your praises among the
 nations!
For your mercy towers to the heavens,
and your faithfulness to the skies.
Be exalted above the heavens, O God,
and your glory be above all the earth.
The full Antiphon: Holy Virgin Mary,
there is none like you. . . .

# Tierce

*The Antiphon intoned:*
*Holy Virgin Mary*

*Shout joyfully to the Lord, all the earth!*
*Sing to the glory of his name!*
*Proclaim his glorious praise.*
*Say to God: How awesome are your*
  *works, O Lord!*
*Because of your mighty power*
*Your enemies will praise you*
  *unwillingly.*
*Let all the earth worship you and sing*
  *praise to you,*
*let it sing a psalm to your name.*
*Come, listen, and I will declare, all you*
  *who fear God,*
*what great things he has done for my*
  *soul.*
*I cried to him with my mouth,*
*and I exulted with the tip of my tongue.*

*And he heard my voice from his holy*
    *temple,*
*and my cry reached his presence.*
*Bless our Lord, you peoples,*
*and make the voice of his praise be*
    *heard.*
*In him shall all the tribes of the earth*
    *be blessed,*
*All nations shall glorify him!*
*Blessed be the Lord, the God of Israel,*
*Who alone does wondrous deeds!*
*And blessed be the name of his majesty*
    *forever,*
*and the whole earth shall be filled with*
    *his majesty:*
*Amen, so be it!*
*The full Antiphon: Holy Virgin Mary,*
*there is none like you. . . .*

# Sext

*The Antiphon intoned:*
*Holy Virgin Mary*

*May the Lord hear you in the day of
   tribulation.*
*May the name of the God of Jacob
   protect you.*
*May he send you help from his holy
   place,*
*and from Zion may he defend you.*
*May he remember all your sacrifices,*
*and may your burnt offerings please
   him.*
*May he grant you what is in your heart*
*and confirm your every plan.*
*We shall rejoice in your victory,*
*and in the name of the Lord our God we
   shall be elated.*
*May the Lord fulfill all you ask of him!*
*Now I know that the Lord has sent*

Jesus Christ his Son
and that he shall judge the peoples in
    justice.
And the Lord has become the refuge of
    the poor,
a helper in times of distress.
And let them hope in you who have
    known your name.
Blessed be the Lord my God,
for he has become my support and my
    refuge
in the day of my trouble.
My helper, I shall sing to you,
because you are God, my defense,
my God, my mercy.
The full Antiphon: Holy Virgin Mary,
there is none like you. . . .

# Nones

*The Antiphon intoned:*
*Holy Virgin Mary*

*In you, O Lord, I have hoped;*
*let me never be put to shame.*
*In your justice rescue me and deliver*
*me.*
*Incline your ear to me,*
*and save me.*
*Be unto me a God, a protector,*
*a stronghold to give me safety.*
*For you are my hope, O Lord,*
*My trust, O Lord, from my youth.*
*On you have I depended since birth;*
*from my mother's womb you are my*
*Protector,*
*and of you shall I continually sing.*
*Let my mouth be filled with praise,*
*that I may sing your glory,*
*and all the day long your greatness.*

*Hear me, O Lord, for your mercy is kind;*
*look upon me according to the bounty*
*of your kindness.*
*And turn not your face away from your*
*servant!*
*Because I am in trouble, hear me*
*quickly!*
*Blessed be the Lord my God,*
*for he has become my support and my*
*refuge*
*in the day of my distress.*
*O my helper, I will sing your praise,*
*for God is my support!*
*My God, my mercy!*
*The full Antiphon: Holy Virgin Mary,*
*there is none like you. . . .*

# The Office
# of the Passion

**Christmastide**
From Vespers on Christmas Eve to the Octave
of Epiphany according to the direction of Saint
Francis, the following psalm is said at all the
Hours. It should be prefaced by the "Praises to
Be Said at Each Hour of the Office." Then the
Antiphon, Holy Virgin Mary, is intoned and
the psalm follows.

The Antiphon intoned: Holy Virgin Mary

# The Psalm

*Sing joyfully to God our strength!*
*Shout to the Lord God living and true*
*with cries of gladness!*
*For the Lord, the most high, the*
*    awesome,*
*is the great King over all the earth.*
*Because the most holy Father of*
*heaven,*
*our King before all ages,*
*sent his beloved Son from on high;*
*and he was born of the blessed Virgin*
*    Mary.*
*He cried out to me: you are my Father!*
*and I will make him the firstborn,*
*high above the kings of the earth.*
*On that day the Lord bestowed his*
*    mercy,*
*and at night I have his song.*
*This is the day the Lord has made:*
*let us be glad and rejoice therein.*

For the most holy beloved Child is
     given to us,
and was born for us on the way and was
     laid in a manger,
because there was no room in the inn.
Glory to the Lord God in the highest,
and on earth peace to men of good will.
Let the heavens be glad and the earth
     rejoice;
let the sea and all that fills it resound;
let the plains be joyful and all that is in
     them.
Sing to the Lord a new song,
sing to the Lord, all the earth!
For great is the Lord and highly to be
     praised,
awesome is he, beyond all gods.
Give to the Lord, you families of
     nations,
give to the Lord glory and honor;
give to the Lord the honor due his
     name.
Offer up your bodies and carry his cross,
and observe his most holy
     commandments to the very end.
Let us bless the Lord God living and
     true;

let us always render to him praise, glory,
  honor,
blessing, and all good things. Amen,
Amen.
The full Antiphon: Holy Virgin Mary,
there is none like you. . . .

# The Office
# of the Passion

**Sundays of the Year**
For Sundays of the year (after Epiphany to Palm
Sunday inclusive); for Holy Thursday; and from
the Octave of Pentecost (now Holy Trinity) to
the Last Sunday before Advent; and on the
principal Feasts which occur in such parts of
the liturgical year.

# Matins

*The Antiphon intoned:*
*Holy Virgin Mary*

*Sing a new song unto the Lord,*
*for he has done wondrous deeds.*
*His right hand and his holy arm*
*has sacrificed his beloved Son.*
*The Lord has made his salvation*
  *known:*
*in the sight of the nations he has*
  *revealed his justice.*
*On that day the Lord bestowed his*
  *mercy:*
*and at night I have his song.*
*This is the day the Lord has made:*
*let us be glad and rejoice in it.*
*Blessed is he who comes in the name of*
  *the Lord:*
*the Lord is God, and he has shone upon*
  *us.*

Let the heavens be glad and the earth
　　rejoice,
let the sea and all that fills it resound:
let the plains be joyful and all that is in
　　them.
Give to the Lord, you families of
　　nations,
give to the Lord glory and praise:
give to the Lord the glory due his name!
The full Antiphon: Holy Virgin Mary,
　　there is none like you. . . .

# Prime

*The Antiphon intoned:*
*Holy Virgin Mary*

*Have mercy on me, O God, have mercy*
*    on me:*
*for my soul trusts in you.*
*And in the shadow of your wings I will*
*    hope,*
*until iniquity pass away.*
*I will call to my most holy Father, the*
*    most high,*
*to the Lord who has done good to me.*
*He has sent from heaven and freed me:*
*He has made those a reproach who*
*    trampled on me.*
*God has sent his mercy and*
*    faithfulness:*
*He has snatched my soul from my*
*    mighty enemies*
*and from those who hated me,*

for they were too powerful for me.
They have prepared a snare for my feet,
and have bowed down my soul.
They have dug a pit before my face,
and they have fallen into it.
My heart is steadfast, O God! My heart
is steadfast!
I will sing and chant a psalm of praise.
Awake, my soul; awake lyre and harp!
I will awake the dawn.
I will give praise to you among the
peoples, O Lord!
I will chant your praise among the
nations!
For your mercy towers to the heavens,
and your faithfulness to the skies.
Be exalted above the heavens, O God,
and your glory be above all the earth.
The full Antiphon: Holy Virgin Mary,
there is none like you. . . .

# Tierce

The Antiphon intoned:
*Holy Virgin Mary*

*Shout joyfully to the Lord, all the earth!*
*Sing to the glory of his name!*
*Proclaim his glorious praise!*
*Say to God: How awesome are your*
    *works, O Lord.*
*Because of your mighty strength*
*your enemies will praise you*
    *unwillingly.*
*Let all the earth worship you and sing*
    *praise to you,*
*let it sing a psalm to your name.*
*Come, listen, and I will declare, all you*
    *who fear God,*
*what great things he has done for my*
    *soul.*
*I cried to him in words,*
*and praise was on the tip of my tongue.*

And from his holy temple he heard my
    voice,
and my cry reached his presence.
Bless our Lord, you peoples,
and make the voice of his praise be
    heard.
And in him shall all the tribes of the
    earth be blessed.
All nations shall glorify him.
Blessed be the Lord, the God of Israel,
who alone does wondrous deeds.
And blessed be the name of his majesty
forever,
and the whole earth shall be filled with
his majesty:
Amen! So be it!
The full Antiphon: Holy Virgin Mary,
there is none like you. . . .

# Sext

*The Antiphon intoned:*
*Holy Virgin Mary*

*May the Lord hear you in the day of*
  *tribulation.*
*May the name of the God of Jacob*
  *protect you.*
*May he send you help from his holy*
  *place,*
*and from Zion may he defend you.*
*May he remember all your sacrifices,*
*and may your burnt offerings please*
  *him.*
*May he grant you what is in your heart,*
*and confirm your every plan.*
*We shall rejoice in your victory,*
*and in the name of the Lord our God we*
  *shall be elated.*
*May the Lord fulfill all you ask of him!*
*Now I know that the Lord has sent*

Jesus Christ his Son
and that he shall judge the peoples in
   justice.
And the Lord has become the refuge of
   the poor,
a helper in times of distress.
And let them hope in you who have
known your name.
Blessed be the Lord my God,
for he has become my support and my
refuge
in the day of my trouble.
My helper, I shall sing to you,
because you are God my defense.
My God, my mercy!
The full Antiphon: Holy Virgin Mary,
there is none like you. . . .

# Nones

The Antiphon intoned:
*Holy Virgin Mary*

In you, O Lord, I have hoped;
let me never be put to shame.
In your justice rescue me and deliver
   me.
Incline your ear to me, and save me.
Be unto me a God, a protector,
a stronghold to give me safety.
For you are my hope, O Lord,
my trust, O Lord, from my youth.
On you I depend from birth;
from my mother's womb you are my
   protector,
and of you shall I continually sing.
Let my mouth be filled with praise,
that I may sing your glory,
and all the day long your greatness.
Hear me, O Lord, for your mercy is kind;

*look upon me according to the bounty*
*of your kindness.*
*And turn not your face away from your*
*servant!*
*Because I am in trouble, hear me*
*quickly!*
*Blessed be the Lord my God,*
*for he has become my support and my*
*refuge*
*in the day of my distress.*
*O my helper, I will sing your praise,*
*for God is my support!*
*My God, my mercy!*
*The full Antiphon: Holy Virgin Mary,*
*there is none like you. . . .*

# Vespers

The Antiphon intoned:
Holy Virgin Mary

All you people, clap your hands:
shout to God with cries of gladness!
For the Lord, the most high, the
    awesome,
is the great King over all the earth.
Because of the most holy Father of
    heaven,
our King before all ages,
sent his beloved Son from on high,
and has wrought salvation in the midst
    of the earth.
Let the heavens be glad and the earth
    rejoice:
let the sea and all that fills it be moved;
let the plains be joyful and all things
    that are in them.
Sing to the Lord a new song;

Sing to the Lord, all you lands!
For great is the Lord and highly to be
    praised;
awesome is he, beyond all gods.
Give to the Lord, you families of
    nations;
give to the Lord glory and honor:
give to the Lord the glory due his name.
Offer up your bodies and carry his holy
    cross
and follow to the very end his most
    holy precepts.
Let all the earth tremble before him.
Say among the nations that the Lord has
    reigned from the cross.
[On the feast of the Ascension we are to
add:
And he ascended into heaven and is
    seated
at the right hand of the most holy
    Father in heaven:
Be exalted above the heavens, O God;
above all the earth be your glory!
And we know that he is coming,
for he will come to judge justice.]
The full Antiphon: Holy Virgin Mary,
there is none like you. . . .

# The Office
# of the Passion

**Ordinary Weekdays**
For weekdays from the Octave of Epiphany to
Holy Saturday (except Holy Thursday); and
from Trinity Sunday to the Saturday before
Advent.

# *Matins*

The Antiphon intoned:
*Holy Virgin Mary*

*O Lord, the God of my salvation,*
*by day I cry out,*
*and in the night I clamor in your*
  *presence.*
*Let my prayer come before you:*
*incline your ear to my call for help.*
*Attend to my soul and deliver it:*
*Because of my enemies snatch me away.*
*For it was you who drew me out of the*
  *womb:*
*My security at the breasts of my*
  *mother;*
*To you was I committed from the*
  *womb.*
*From my mother's womb you are my*
  *God:*
*O be not far from me.*

You know my reproach and my
    confusion,
and my ignominy.
In your sight are all those who afflict
    me;
my heart has expected such reproach
    and misery.
And I looked for one who would grieve
    with me,
and there was no one!
And for one who would comfort me, and
    I found none.
O God, the wicked have risen against
    me
and the company of the powerful seek
    my life,
nor do they set you before their eyes.
I am numbered with those who go down
    into the pit:
I have become as a man without help,
    free among the dead.
You are my most holy Father,
my King and my God.
Make haste to help me,
O Lord, the God of my salvation.
The full Antiphon: Holy Virgin Mary,
there is none like you. . . .

# Prime

The Antiphon intoned:
Holy Virgin Mary

Have mercy on me, O God, have mercy
    on me:
for my soul trusts in you.
And in the shadow of your wings I will
    hope,
until iniquity pass away.
I will call to my most holy Father, the
    most high,
to the Lord who has done good to me.
He has sent from heaven and freed me:
He has made those a reproach who
    trampled on me.
God has sent his mercy and his
    faithfulness:
He has snatched my soul from my
    mighty enemies
and from those who hated me,

for they were too powerful for me.
They have prepared a snare for my feet,
and have bowed down my soul.
They have dug a pit before my face,
and have fallen into it.
My heart is steadfast, O God! My heart
   is steadfast!
I will sing and chant a psalm of praise.
Awake my soul! Awake lyre and harp!
I will awake the dawn!
I will give praise to you among the
   peoples, O Lord!
I will chant your praise among the
   nations!
For your mercy towers to the heavens,
and your faithfulness to the skies.
Be exalted above the heavens, O God,
and your glory be above all the earth.
The full Antiphon: Holy Virgin Mary,
there is none like you. . . .

# Tierce

The Antiphon intoned:
Holy Virgin Mary

Have pity on me, O God, for men
    trample on me;
all day long they press their attack
    against me.
My enemies have trampled on me all
    the day,
for they are many who make war
    against me.
All my enemies have devised evil
    against me,
and imagine the worst against me.
Those who keep watch against my life
have taken counsel together,
they have gone forth and whispered
    against me.
All who see me scoff at me;
they mock me with parted lips and wag

their heads.
I am a worm, and not a man,
the scorn of men and the outcast of the
    people.
For all my enemies I am an object of
    reproach,
a laughing-stock to my neighbors,
and a dread to those who know me.
Holy Father, let not your help be far
    from me,
but rather look to my defense.
Make haste to help me,
O Lord God of my salvation!
The full Antiphon: Holy Virgin Mary,
there is none like you. . . .

# Sext

The Antiphon intoned:
Holy Virgin Mary

With a loud voice I cried to the Lord;
with a loud voice I besought the
    Lord.
My complaint I pour out before him;
before him I lay bare my distress.
When my spirit was faint within me,
you have known my paths.
In the way on which I was walking
the proud ones hid a snare for me.
I looked to the right to see,
and there was no one who would pay
    me heed.
I had lost all means of escape,
and there was no one who cared for my
    life.
Since for your sake I have borne insult,
shame has covered my face!

I have become an outcast to my
    brothers,
and a stranger to the sons of my mother.
Holy Father, zeal for your house
    consumes me,
and the insults of those
who blaspheme you fall on me.
And they rejoiced against me and
    gathered together,
heaping blows upon me when I did not
    expect them.
Those outnumber the hairs of my head
who hate me without cause.
They have grown strong, my enemies
who hate me without cause:
Must I restore what I did not steal?
Unjust witnesses have risen up
and asked me things they did not know.
They repaid me evil for good and
    harassed me
because I pursued goodness.
You are my most holy Father,
my King and my God!
Make haste to help me,
O Lord, the God of my salvation!
The full Antiphon: Holy Virgin Mary,
    there is none like you. . . .

# Nones

*The Antiphon intoned:*
*Holy Virgin Mary*

*O all you that pass by the way,*
*attend and see if there is any sorrow*
     *like my sorrow.*
*For many dogs have surrounded me,*
*a pack of evildoers has closed in upon*
     *me.*
*They have looked on and gloated over*
     *me.*
*They have divided my garments among*
     *them,*
*and for my vesture they cast lots.*
*They have pierced my hands and my*
     *feet,*
*and have counted all my bones.*
*They have opened their mouths against*
     *me,*
*like ravening and roaring lions.*

*I am poured out like water,*
*and all my bones are racked.*
*And my heart has become like wax*
*melting away within my bosom.*
*My throat is dried up like baked*
   *clay,*
*and my tongue cleaves to my jaws.*
*And they gave me gall for my food,*
*and in my thirst they gave me vinegar*
   *to drink.*
*And they brought me down into the*
   *dust of death,*
*and added to the grief of my wounds.*
*I have slept and I have risen again,*
*and my most holy Father has received*
   *me with glory.*
*Holy Father, you have held my right*
   *hand*
*and have guided me with your counsel,*
*and with glory have lifted me up.*
*For what else have I in heaven,*
*and apart from you what have I desired*
   *upon earth?*
*See, see, that I am God, says the Lord!*
*And I will be exalted among the nations*
*and I will be exalted upon the earth.*
*Blessed be the Lord the God of Israel,*

who has redeemed the souls of his
  servants
by his own most precious blood,
and will not abandon all who hope in
him.
And we know that he is coming,
for he will come to judge justice.
The full Antiphon: Holy Virgin Mary,
there is none like you. . . .

# Vespers

*The Antiphon intoned:*
*Holy Virgin Mary*

*All you peoples, clap your hands:*
*Shout to God with cries of gladness!*
*For the Lord, the most high, the*
   *awesome,*
*is the great King over all the earth.*
*Because the most holy Father of heaven,*
*our King before all ages,*
*sent his beloved Son from on high,*
*and has wrought salvation in the midst*
   *of the earth.*
*Let the heavens be glad and the earth*
   *rejoice;*
*let the sea and all that fills it be moved;*
*let the plains be joyful*
*and all things that are in them.*
*Sing to the Lord a new song;*
*sing to the Lord, all you lands!*

For great is the Lord and highly to be
   praised:
Awesome is he, beyond all gods.
Give to the Lord, you families of
   nations;
give to the Lord glory and honor:
give to the Lord the glory due his name!
Offer your bodies and carry his holy
   cross,
and follow to the very end his most
holy precepts and commandments.
Let all the earth tremble before him.
Say among the nations
that the Lord has reigned from the cross.
[On the feast of the Ascension add this
verse:
And he ascended into heaven
and is seated at the right hand
of the most holy Father in heaven:
Be exalted above the heavens, O God;
above all the earth be your glory.
And we know that he is coming,
for he will come to judge justice.]
The full Antiphon: Holy Virgin Mary,
there is none like you. . . .

# Compline

*The Antiphon intoned:*
*Holy Virgin Mary*

*O God, I have declared to you my life;*
*my tears you have placed in your sight.*
*All my enemies were devising evil*
  *against me*
*and took counsel together.*
*They repaid me evil for good,*
*and hatred for my love.*
*In return for my love they slandered me,*
*but I gave myself to prayer.*
*My holy Father,*
*King of heaven and earth,*
*be not far from me,*
*for distress is near, and there is no one*
  *to help me.*
*May my enemies be turned back;*
*in whatever day I shall call upon you,*
*behold I know you are my God.*

My friends and my companions stand
  back
because of my affliction,
and my neighbors stand afar off.
You have taken my friends away from
  me:
You have made me an abomination to
  them;
I have been betrayed, and I cannot
  escape.
Holy Father, let your help be not far
  from me;
my God, come to my aid.
Make haste to help me, O Lord,
the God of my salvation.
Glory to the Father and to the Son
and to the Holy Spirit.
As it was in the beginning,
is now, and ever shall be, world without
  end. Amen!
The full Antiphon: Holy Virgin Mary,
there is none like you. . . .

# The Office
# of the Passion

**Concluding Prayer**
The concluding prayer to this Office at the
end of Compline is as follows:

*Let us bless the Lord God living and
true! Let us always render him praise,
glory, honor, blessing, and all good
things! Amen. Amen. So be it! So be it!*

## *Also of Interest from Servant Publications*

### St. Francis of Assisi
A Biography
*By Omer Englebert*

*An acclaimed work of modern scholarship which is also a timeless popular work of inspiring spiritual reading.*
$4.95 (paperback)

### The Little Flowers of St. Francis
Incorporating the Acts of St. Francis and His Companions
*Translated by E.M. Blaiklock and A.C. Keys*

A new translation of this popular, inspirational classic.
$4.95 (paperback)

Available at your Christian bookstore or from:
**Servant Publications • Dept. 209 • P.O. Box 7455
Ann Arbor, Michigan 48107**
Please include payment plus $1.25 per book
for postage and handling.
*Send for our FREE catalog of Christian
books, music, and cassettes.*